Angel Over Me

Written by Ruth and Miriam Rieder
Illustrated by Wes Comer

ANGELS WATCHING OVER ME
KINGDOM KIDS SERIES
Written by: Ruth and Miriam Rieder

Dedicated to all the Kingdom Kids around the world. My humble desire is that somehow these writings would establish and anchor the truth of holiness within the hearts and minds of the younger generation. **"And that from a child thou hast known the holy scriptures, which are able to make thee wise unto salvation through faith which is in Christ Jesus."** (II Timothy 3:15) In a day of non-commitment and trashing of godly values may they **"Buy the truth, and sell it not; also wisdom, and instruction, and understanding."** (Proverbs 23:23)

All text and images copyright © 2002 Ruth Rieder

ISBN#: 0-9674360-5-2

First Printing March 2002
5000 copies

Illustrated by Wes Comer
Design by Comertoons Illustration & Design

Unless otherwise indicated, all Scripture quotations are taken from the King James Version of the Bible.

For information contact:
Ruth Rieder
PO Box 15252
Rio Rancho, NM 87174

Please visit our Web Site @ www.positivepowerofholiness.com
On-line ordering and credit charging available for all products at this address

TABLE OF CONTENTS:
Angels Watching Over Me
Kingdom Kid's Quiz #1
Kingdom Kid's Quiz #2
Kingdom Kid's Bible Memorization
Order Form

The bright morning sun filtered through the light green window shade in Miriam's bedroom as she snuggled deeper under the warm covers. The noise of clattering breakfast dishes and the *swish-swish* of the washing machine echoed in the distance. Miriam buried her head under the pillow. She would love to sleep another hour.

Outside her door, like a little alarm clock sat her precious little fur ball, a kitten named Ashes. He was completely black except for a white bow tie and three white spots on his underside. His bright golden-green eyes watched expectantly for Mother to come up the stairs and wake Miriam for another day of school. He purred softly as his tail switched from side to side.

When the sound of footsteps came up the stairs, Ashes stretched lazily and walked over to the door. Cheerfully Mother called out, "Hey, beautiful girl, it's time to get up!" Inwardly Miriam groaned and pretended to be asleep. Mother opened the door and Ashes jumped on Miriam's bed. He stuck his wet nose in her ear and purred all the louder. Slowly her bright blue eyes opened as Mother sat on the side of her bed.

Stroking her light blonde hair, Mother began praying for Miriam before she started her day. **"Lord Jesus, watch over Miriam as she goes to school today. Put a hedge of protection around her and allow no harm to come to her. Let the angels of the Lord encamp about her and cover her with the armor of God. May her loins be girt with truth, her heart protected with the breastplate of righteousness, and her feet shod with the preparation of the gospel of peace. Above all, let her take the shield of faith to quench all the fiery darts of the wicked. Guard her mind with the helmet of salvation and give her skill with the sword of the Spirit which is the Word of God.** (Ephesians 6:13-17) **Help her to be a woman of prayer, a mighty woman of God. Thank you for another beautiful day to serve You. We love you Jesus! In Jesus' Name, Amen!"**

As Mother stepped into the closet, Miriam questioned her. "Mommy, why do you pray for me every morning?" "Because we live in a scary world and need Jesus to watch over us every minute of the day," replied Mother. "It isn't safe out there without Him beside us all the time." Miriam thought about that and then asked, "What is a "hedge of protection?" "It is a fence of safety God puts around us," answered Mother. "His fence keeps good things in and bad things out."

Coming out of the closet with some clothes in her hand, she began helping Miriam into her school uniform, a white blouse, navy skirt and tights. "Just like your school has a uniform, God has a special uniform made to protect every part of your body. It is called the armor of God and should be worn daily. First of all you wrap yourself in truth. Next your heart is covered with righteousness which is the power to do right."

When Mother paused to button Miriam's blouse, the little girl quickly asked, "What does "shod" mean? That is a funny word!" "'Shod' means to put on shoes. You are to put on the shoes of peace. It is so important to get along with others. When you do this your light shines for Jesus," said Mother as Miriam slipped on her school shoes.

Eager to know more, Miriam continued to ask questions. "What is the 'shield of faith' and how does it quench darts? Are you talking about a dart game?" "No, it is much more than a dart game," said Mother. "Back in the Bible days, the Roman soldiers carried large shields to protect their bodies. It was part of their armor. Before a battle, the leather shields were soaked in water. The wet shields were used to quench or put out the flaming arrows thrown at them by the enemy. Faith in God is like a soldier's shield. It protects you from the devil's darts when he tries to throw lies, fear, hate, and other bad things your way."

"After you take the shield of faith, the helmet of salvation is placed on your head. This protects your mind from bad thoughts and scary dreams. Finally you take up the sword of the Spirit which is the Word of God. The Bible is your weapon and will protect you when satan tempts you to sin. King David said, "Thy word have I hid in mine heart, that I might not sin against thee." (Psalm 119:11)"

Glancing at the clock, Mother said, "It's 8:15. Go wash your face and I will comb your hair." When Miriam turned on the water, Ashes bounded into the bathroom and jumped on the counter. He batted the water with his paws then knocked the sink stopper around. That was his way of saying he was thirsty. Miriam ran some water in the sink and Ashes slurped it up.

13

After Miriam washed her face, Mother began to brush her hair. The little girl said, "My friend, Samantha just got her hair cut. Now all the kids at school are asking me why I don't cut my hair. So I told them it was because of my religion." Mother paused and looked at her daughter. "Miriam, there is a much greater reason than religion. We do not cut our hair because God's Word commands the woman to have long hair. Our obedience brings a wonderful promise of protection. Like the armor of God, our uncut hair also creates a covering of safety for us and our families."

"For this cause ought the woman to have power on her head because of the angels." (I Corinthians 11:10)

Continuing to brush her child's silky blonde hair, Mother said, "You have power on your head because of the angels. That means there are big strong angels watching over you all the time. I like to call them "Angelic Bodyguards."

"What are bodyguards?" asked Miriam. "A bodyguard is a person who is responsible for the physical safety of someone," replied Mother. " All important people such as presidents, kings or queens have many bodyguards who carry guns and watch over them. You are important too because your heavenly Father is the King of Kings. That makes you a King's Kid, a spiritual royal princess with angelic bodyguards. They watch over you continually twenty-four hours a day, seven days a week and are with you everywhere you go. You do not ever have to be afraid because **"The angel of the LORD encampeth round about them that fear him, and delivereth them."** (Psalm 34:7)

"What does 'encampeth' mean?" asked Miriam. "It means the angels of God set up a camp or a secure place all around you. Nothing can come close to harm you at any time when you are in the will of God." A big smile spread across Miriam's face as she thought about all the big strong angels taking care of her. She picked up Ashes and held him close and said, "Just think Ashes, we have angelic bodyguards who take care of us." The little black kitten looked at her with his big golden-green eyes and purred contentedly as if he understood everything she told him.

When Mother finished her hair and tied it with a big bow, the little girl said, "I wish my hair was long like Jessica's. Her hair is below her waist and mine only reaches the middle of my back." Mother told her, "The length of your hair is not important. God made every person different. He decides how long your hair grows and what matters to Him is that you never cut the hair created especially for you. Never put scissors to your hair because the Bible says your long hair is a glory to you."

"What does that mean?" questioned Miriam. "Your uncut hair is a visible sign of God's glory resting on your head. That is why all the kids at school ask you about not cutting your hair. Your light is continually shining for Jesus when they see your uncut hair. They know you are different" replied Mother. "Always remember that you are special and your hair is made by God. You are a King's Kid!"

"It's almost 8:30," exclaimed Mother. "You must hurry and eat your breakfast so you are not late to school." Miriam skipped down the stairs as she hummed to herself, "I'm a King's Kid and I have angels watching over me!" Ashes ran down the stairs like a little shadow right beside her. When Miriam sat down at the kitchen table, Ashes hopped up on her lap. He wanted to eat breakfast with her. So he stuck his nose in her plate and tried to lick the cream cheese off of her bagel. "Ashes Rieder, get your nose out of my food!" squealed Miriam. Jumping down, Ashes went running into the laundry room to lick the cream cheese off of his nose.

While Miriam ate her grapefruit and bagel, she continued to ask her Mother more questions. "What about boys? Is their hair supposed to be long or short?" Mother pulled up a chair at the table and sat down as she continued to explain God's wonderful Word. "The Bible tells us the men and boys are to have short hair." "Why?" asked the curious child. "Because they represent God and are supposed to look like Him," replied Mother.

"Boys with long hair really look funny," giggled

21

Miriam. "It always makes me laugh and think they are silly." Mother told her, "God made you feel that way because His Word says, **"Doth not even nature itself teach you, that, if a man have long hair, it is a shame unto him?"** (I Corinthians 11:14) "In the sight of God it is shameful for men and boys to have long hair. God never intended for boys to look like girls with long hair and ponytails or girls to look like boys with their hair all chopped off. In His Kingdom, the boys look like boys and the girls look like girls!" "So are the boys King's Kids too?" asked Miriam. "Yes they are if they obey God," said Mother. "They are spiritual royal princes and represent the King of Kings."

"It is really special to be God's kid, isn't it, Mom," said Miriam as she finished up her breakfast. "It is the most wonderful privilege on earth. Do not ever be ashamed of being a King's Kid. Hold your head high and rejoice in who you are. Your Heavenly Father is the King of Kings - that makes you special!" replied Mother. Just then Dad walked in and said, "It's time to leave for school." Miriam ran to get her blue lunch bag and backpack. She gave Mother a hug and said, "Mom, take good care of

Ashes today. Please don't let him outside because he might get hurt." Picking up her kitten, the little girl held him close, whispering in his ear, "Ashes, don't forget about God's armor and the angels. We learned a lot today. She hugged him one last time and ran out the door. "Have a wonderful day," Mother called out, "and remember you are a King's Kid. There are 'Angels watching over you' today!"

"For this cause ought the woman to have power on her head because of the angels."
(I Corinthians 11:10)

"For he shall give his angels charge over thee, to keep thee in all thy ways."

(Psalm 91:11)

Kingdom Kids Quiz # 1:

1. Why should we pray every morning?
2. What is a 'hedge of protection'?
3. What is God's special uniform?
4. When should it be worn?
5. What does it protect?
6. "First of all you wrap yourself in _____?"
7. What covers your heart?
8. What does 'shod' mean?
9. What kind of shoes are you supposed to wear?
10. Why did the Roman soldiers carry shields?
11. Was it part of their armor?
12. Before the battle what did they soak the leather shields in?
13. Why did they soak the shields?
14. The soldier's shield is like _____ __ _____.
15. What are some of the devil's darts?
16. What do you wear on your head?
17. What does it protect you from?
18. What is your weapon?
19. When does it protect you?
20. Why do we hide God's Word in our hearts?

27

Kingdom Kids Quiz # 2:

1. Is religion the reason women are not supposed to cut their hair?
2. What commands the woman to have long hair?
3. Obedience brings a _____ _____ _____ _____.
4. Uncut hair creates a covering of _____.
5. The woman has power on her head because of what?
6. What is watching over you all the time
7. Our heavenly Father is the _____ of _____.
8. That makes you a _____ _____.
9. How often does God's angels watch over you?
10. Who decides how long a girl's hair grows?
11. Is every person different?
12. Do not ever put a _____ to your hair.
13. Your long hair is a _____ to you.
14. Are boys supposed to have long or short hair?
15. Who are boys supposed to look like?
16. Do you think boys with long hair look funny?
17. Who made you feel that way?
18. Are boys King's Kids too if they obey God's Word?
19. What is the most wonderful privilege on earth?
20. Are King's Kids special?

Kingdom Kids Bible Memorization: Find the following Bible verses in the book and memorize them.

Psalm 119:11
I Corinthians 11:10
Psalm 34:7
Psalm 91:11
I Corinthians 11:14
II Timothy 3:15
Proverbs 23:23

Advanced Kingdom Kids Bible Memorization:

Ephesians 6:13-17

Other Titles Available from Ruth Rieder

Kingdom Kids Series	Qty	Price	Ext.
Book #1: Angels Watching Over Me		$6.00	
Book #2: Kingdom Clothing		$6.00	
Book #3: Marble Palaces or Painted Barns		$6.00	
Book #4: God's Jewels		$6.00	

The Positive Power of Holiness Study Curriculum	Qty	Price	Ext
Power Before the Throne		$9.00	
Reflecting the Glory		$10.00	
The Positive Power of Holiness (Interactive study guide for Power Before the Throne and Reflecting the Glory)		$12.00	
Student Test Pack (14 comprehensive tests)		$7.00	
Teacher Test Pack (14 test score keys)		$7.00	
The Positive Power of Holiness Teaching Video		$22.00	
The Positive Power of Holiness Audio Cassette		$11.00	
'Keys To Knowing God' Prayer and Fasting Series	Qty	Price	Ext
Prayer = Relationship		$9.00	
Building Prayer Equity		$9.00	
Biblical Fasting		$9.00	
Other Books and Tapes	Qty	Price	Ext
Covenant by Sacrifice		$11.00	

Name_____

Address_____

City _____ State_____ Zip Code_____

Phone # _____ email_____

All prices include shipping. Please make checks payable to Living Word Publications, and send order along with payment to:
P.O. Box 15252
Rio Rancho, NM 87174.